heaven
on
earth

heaven on earth

A Guided Journal for Creating Your Own Divine Paradise

TANYA RICHARDSON

This book is dedicated to my grandmothers,
Theda and Marguerite

An Imprint of Sterling Publishing
387 Park Avenue South
New York, NY 10016

ISBN 978-1-4549-1339-9

Distributed in Canada by Sterling Publishing
c/o Canadian Manda Group, 165 Dufferin Street
Toronto, Ontario, Canada M6K 3H6
Distributed in the United Kingdom by GMC Distribution Services
Castle Place, 166 High Street, Lewes, East Sussex, England BN7 1XU
Distributed in Australia by Capricorn Link (Australia) Pty. Ltd.
P.O. Box 704, Windsor, NSW 2756, Australia

For information about custom editions, special sales, and premium and corporate purchases, please contact Sterling Special Sales at 800-805-5489 or specialsales@sterlingpublishing.com.

Manufactured in China

2 4 6 8 10 9 7 5 3 1

www.sterlingpublishing.com

contents

introduction

You probably think of heaven as a place where:

You are surrounded by love.
Anything is possible.
Everything is beautiful.
You are forgiven.
You are your best self.
Angels watch over you.
Peace is with you.
Your heart is free.

Just reading that list makes me almost eager to get to heaven. When people who have had near-death experiences talk about the ultimate love and peace they encounter on the other side, we often feel like all we can do is politely listen in ignorant awe. But do we really have to wait a whole lifetime, or even a single moment, to experience overwhelming peace and love? Maybe if we start thinking about concepts like "anything is possible" or "your heart is free" right now, in the process we can create our own "heaven" on earth.

In *Heaven on Earth* you'll discover the divine things, people, places, and ideas that already surround you in abundance. And you'll craft a personalized list of these ethereal things, people, places, and ideas. That way whenever you catch yourself feeling curious about what heaven is really like, you can open your copy of *Heaven on Earth* and realize that you're already there.

"Whenever we manage to
love without expectations,
calculations, negotiations,
we are indeed in heaven."

— RUMI

CHAPTER 1

in heaven. . . you are surrounded by love

The phrase "surrounded by love" implies that love is everywhere, to the extent that our hearts are unable to feel any other emotion. When we get a big hug from a family member who hasn't seen us for a while, or when we hug a friend who's going through a hard time, the force of love in our arms totally blocks out, at least for a few precious moments, any other emotion. We actually feel surrounded by love.

Dogs pile on top of each other to take a nap, and even sea otters hold hands while they float through the water. Human animals are no different: touch not only improves our mood, it boosts our immune system. Touch isn't just something we like—it's something we *need* in order to achieve heaven on earth.

Do you know someone who gives supersized hugs?

FAMILY MEMBERS:

____

____

____

____

FRIENDS:

COWORKERS:

Who can you go to for a hug when you need to feel loved?

FAMILY MEMBERS WHO LIVE NEARBY:

FRIENDS WHO LIVE NEARBY:

COWORKERS IN YOUR OFFICE:

Who might need a big, surrounded-by-love hug from you right now?

What are some of the most memorable hugs you have received?

If you could give anyone a hug right now (even if that person has passed on or lives on the other side of the world), who would it be?

HOW CAN YOU SHOW THAT PERSON YOU LOVE THEM WITHOUT PUTTING YOUR ARMS AROUND THEM?

How does receiving a loving touch make you feel? (examples: cared for, safe, comforted, happy)

Do you ever visit a massage therapist? Are massages a treat or something you do on a regular basis?

If you have animals as pets, how do they show you physical affection?

The simplest way to feel surrounded by love is to love yourself. No matter whom we're with or what we're doing, we can't escape ourselves. So when we want to feel a pervasive love, the quickest route is the most obvious.

If our hearts crave love in the form of self-confidence, we might reflect on past achievements. If our hearts long for love in the form of nurturing, we can listen to soothing music or order in our favorite meal. If our hearts call out for love in the form of assistance, we can ask a coworker or partner or health-care professional for help.

Instead of holding a grudge against yourself, forgive yourself for past mistakes. Instead of making life a punishment, actively seek out joy and comfort each day. Instead of abandoning yourself in a crisis, make your needs a priority even when you are in the role of caregiver. The better we become at loving ourselves, the better we become at creating heaven on earth.

{ there really are endless ways to tell yourself "i love you." }

How can you tell yourself "I love you" today?

What are some accomplishments you are proud of?

Whom can you ask for help or advice if you are feeling overwhelmed?

AT HOME:

AT WORK:

HEALTH-CARE PROFESSIONAL(S):

What project or chore could you take off your plate, or hire someone else to perform, so you can have more time to smell the roses?

Do you fill your free time with unimportant busywork when you could be relaxing or playing?

Is there a past mistake you need to forgive yourself for?

What activities or aspects of your life feel punishing?

TAKE A FEW MINUTES AND BRAINSTORM WAYS YOU CAN BRING MORE JOY AND COMFORT TO THESE SPECIFIC AREAS OF YOUR LIFE.

What are your favorite ways to treat yourself?

FAVORITE FOODS:

FAVORITE CLOTHING STORE OR DESIGNER:

FAVORITE OUTDOOR ACTIVITY:

FAVORITE SPA TREATMENTS (REMEMBER, YOU CAN ALWAYS GIVE YOURSELF A MANICURE OR FACIAL TO SAVE MONEY):

If you could set aside an afternoon or even a whole day to pamper yourself and rejuvenate, how would you spend it?

Growing up, how often did your parents or guardians tell you that they loved you? How did they show you they loved you?

HOW HAS THIS INFLUENCED (BOTH POSITIVELY AND NEGATIVELY) THE WAY YOU EXPRESS LOVE TO YOURSELF?

The surest way to feel surrounded by love is to surround yourself with people who care for you. This can be as elaborate as a large family reunion or as easy as dinner and a movie with a pal.

My heart feels surrounded by love when I have old friends over to my home and we reminisce about our glory days together; when I see one of my favorite musicians live in concert and I'm with someone who enjoys their music as much as I do; when I share my fears with a confidant and the strength of our friendship makes me feel safe; when I get my girlfriends together for a book club meeting and we learn more about life and each other during the discussion; when I chat about spirituality and philosophy with my friends from church over coffee after the service; when I catch up in person or on the phone with a family member or friend I've been missing; or when I make a special trip to see a close friend or family member who lives far away. Being with people who are dear to me makes me feel surrounded by love.

The popular "less is more" philosophy is appropriate when discussing certain topics, like environmental conservation and accessorizing an outfit. But it has no place in a conversation about love. Spend more, more, more time with people you care about and you will find yourself in heaven on earth.

What event could you start planning today that will make you feel surrounded by love?

FAMILY MEMBERS AND FRIENDS YOU'D LIKE TO VISIT WHO LIVE FAR AWAY:

FAMILY MEMBERS AND FRIENDS YOU'D LIKE TO SEE WHO LIVE NEARBY:

BABY OR WEDDING SHOWER, GRADUATION OR RETIREMENT PARTY, OR OTHER CELEBRATION OF A MILESTONE IN SOMEONE'S LIFE THAT YOU COULD HELP ORGANIZE:

GUEST LIST FOR A DINNER PARTY YOU CAN PLAN:

UPCOMING CONCERT, WORKSHOP, OR SPORTING EVENT YOU COULD ATTEND WITH A FRIEND:

FRIENDS WHO LIKE THE SAME BOOKS AS YOU:

FRIENDS WHO SHARE YOUR SPIRITUAL BELIEFS:

FRIENDS OR FAMILY YOU'VE BEEN PUTTING OFF CALLING:

FRIENDS OR FAMILY YOU COULD SCHEDULE REGULAR PHONE OR VIDEO CHATS WITH AT THE SAME TIME EACH WEEK OR MONTH:

Which person (people) in your life do you most enjoy spending time with?

Which person (people) in your life give the best advice or are the best listeners?

Which person (people) in your life make you laugh or feel easygoing?

Which family members or friends would you like to feel closer to?

Is there a close friend or family member you owe an apology to?

Do you have an estranged friend or family member? Could you send that person an olive branch, such as a birthday present or a holiday card?

HEAVEN IS WHERE THE HEART IS

HEART THOUGHTS

~exercising our enormous capacity to give and receive love is heaven on earth~

YOUR HEART THOUGHTS ABOUT LOVE:

HEART THOUGHTS ABOUT LOVE FROM YOUR FAVORITE MOVIES, BOOKS, AND SONGS:

HEART THOUGHTS ABOUT LOVE FROM YOUR FRIENDS AND FAMILY:

"Heaven is the decision I must make."

— A COURSE IN MIRACLES

CHAPTER 2

in heaven . . . anything is possible

In high school I did *not* believe "anything is possible," probably because I was facing some of life's harshest realities—like the death of my mother. I wasn't interested in school, except for my journalism and English classes, and I'd been so traumatized my freshman, sophomore, and junior years by my mother's terminal illness that I didn't think much about my future. (Nobody else in my family had the time or emotional energy to think about my future either.) On the last day of my senior year, a teacher took me aside and informed me I hadn't passed one of my science classes and wouldn't graduate. I sat back down at my desk and tried to ignore the other kids when they asked why I was crying.

I spent the summer retaking the science course I'd failed, and with my father's financial help, I soon began attending a local college. I entertained the idea of becoming an English literature major, but it wasn't the safest, easiest, or most lucrative major. Could the same girl who had failed science and her senior year pull it off? For the first time, I asked myself the most important question of my life: Why not?

Luckily, at the adventurous age of nineteen, I couldn't come up with many answers to that question, so English literature became my major. I loved my studies so much that I ended up being president of the English department honor society, and after I got my bachelor of arts degree, I was awarded a position in a master of journalism program in London. I'd never packed up everything I owned and moved to a foreign country before. But, *why not*?

After finishing my master's, I wanted to work as a writer, so my best friend agreed to move with me to New York City. We had no acquaintances there, no job leads, and limited funds, but by that point I'd gotten very comfortable asking myself: Why not? (And at twenty-four, this was still largely a rhetorical question.)

For the past fourteen years, I've made a living in the New York publishing industry. Sometimes it's been far from glamorous. Occasionally it's been beyond my wildest dreams. Of course if I tried to embark upon such a journey now, in my late thirties, I could think of so very many reasons "why not." I suppose that's the trick about remembering that anything is possible: ***Keep asking yourself: Why not? And stay young at heart. A youthful appetite for adventure is heaven on earth.***

What are some of the dreams you said "why not" to in the past?

What dreams do you wish you would or could have said "why not" to in the past?

IS THERE A WAY TO DUST OFF SOME OF THOSE OLD DREAMS AND SAY "WHY NOT" NOW?

What new dream(s) does your heart want to say "why not" to today?

What dreams did you go after that didn't work out but that you gained something from the experience?

Why exactly were you glad you tried, or what did you learn?

What have you accomplished that probably shocked some of your friends and family?

When have you accomplished something that even you found shocking?

Name a time when life bestowed a blessing on you that far exceeded your expectations for the situation.

What are some of the biggest adventures you've been on in your life?

Is there an adventure you went on that seemed terrifying when you first considered it, and now you can't imagine your life without that experience?

One of the most powerful lessons in the infinite possibility of the universe happens when our heart witnesses a miracle.

A friend is diagnosed with cancer at the beginning of her pregnancy, but she goes on to deliver a healthy child and enter remission. A woman with a chronic condition learns to accept her limitations and the help of others with grace and gratitude. A man opens his dream business. In its early days his shop is about to fold, but then he makes a large sale that is just enough money to keep the doors open another month, which is just enough time for his store to become profitable. A widow in her eighties falls in love again for the first time since her husband died thirty years before. A woman who has been divorced three times gets married again, and her fourth marriage lasts for twenty-six years—and counting. A young man's drug addiction causes him to lose his job and the will to live, yet years later he is sober and at the top of his industry.

All of these stories are miraculous. They are also true. I know because I witnessed them. Miracles are dramatic, but they are also the stuff of everyday life. ***Watch for miracles in the lives of those around you, be open to receiving miracles yourself—and you will arrive in heaven on earth.***

What are some of the most memorable miracles from your own life?

What was the most recent miracle in your life?

Name some characteristics of a "miracle," using your own experiences to define the word.

Beginning in childhood, try to count the number of miracles you have personally been blessed with—three, ten, thirty.

When has a miracle in the life of a friend or family member inspired you or touched your heart?

Is there an area of your life, or a relationship you're in, that needs a miracle? Use this space to ask God for a miracle now.

Recall a healing miracle you witnessed.

Recall a financial miracle you witnessed.

Recall a relationship miracle you witnessed.

Recall a career miracle you witnessed.

Do you feel open to receiving miracles in your life right now?

IF YOUR ANSWER IS NO, WHY NOT?

Was there a time when your life felt more miraculous? How were you different then? (examples: more hopeful, more present, more grateful)

Realizing that anything is possible requires the courage to dream really, really big. Maybe you want to change careers, start a family, or buy your first home. Maybe you're dreaming of going back to school or falling in love. Maybe your life is out of control, and you dream of finally seeking help.

Little dreams, like finding the perfect hat to wear to a party or turning in an impressive report to your boss, are like snacks or appetizers for your heart and mind. They give you the fuel to get through the day or even just the moment. But big dreams are the main course. Big dreams satiate your *soul.* Big dreams fill your life for years to come.

Sometimes we're scared to dream big. Big dreams don't always come to pass, so there's the chance we will be disappointed. And big dreams take a lot of hard work, time, and commitment, so they are naturally intimidating. But over the course of a lifetime, everyone sees some of their biggest dreams materialize. ***So allow your heart to dream big. It's the only way those big dreams can come true, and it's the only way to truly experience heaven on earth.***

Name three big dreams you had that came true.

WHO ARE SOME OF THE PEOPLE WHO HELPED YOU REALIZE THESE BIG DREAMS?

HOW DID YOU THANK THESE HELPFUL PEOPLE OR CELEBRATE WITH THEM?

WHAT WERE SOME OF THE METHODS YOU EMPLOYED TO MAKE THESE BIG DREAMS BECOME REALITY? (EXAMPLES: PATIENCE, PERSISTENCE, OPENNESS, ASKING FOR HELP, SEEKING EXPERT ADVICE, TAKING CLASSES, WORKING OVERTIME)

HOW LONG DID YOU WORK ON AND REVISE THESE BIG DREAMS BEFORE THEY CAME TRUE?

Describe how you feel when planning or working toward a big dream (examples: full of energy, inspired, thrilled).

Name one big dream that didn't come true, but in trying to achieve it, you experienced significant personal growth.

Name one big dream that didn't come true but pursuing it led to another big dream that did come true.

Do you have a big dream right now that seems currently out of reach or too intimidating?

IF DOWNSIZED A BIT, OR BROKEN INTO STEPS OR SECTIONS, WOULD THIS BIG DREAM BE WITHIN REACH OR LESS INTIMIDATING?

Who can you go to for help or guidance with this big dream?

HEART THOUGHTS

~heaven on earth is witnessing and participating in miracles~

YOUR HEART THOUGHTS ABOUT POSSIBILITY:

HEART THOUGHTS ABOUT POSSIBILITY FROM YOUR FAVORITE MOVIES, BOOKS, OR SONGS:

HEART THOUGHTS ABOUT POSSIBILITY FROM YOUR FRIENDS AND FAMILY:

"Heaven is under our feet as well as over our heads."

– HENRY DAVID THOREAU

CHAPTER 3

in heaven . . . everything is beautiful

When I walk through one of my favorite parks, into the woods, or along the beach, my heart is overwhelmed by the fact that everywhere I look there is something of beauty. Brilliant sunshine reflecting off the water, colorful wildflowers boldly blooming in spring, delicate feathers on a sparrow, the magic of lightning bugs at dusk. The more time we spend in nature, the more our hearts sense that this planet is the ultimate paradise. There is something about being in nature that is undeniably grounding, undeniably holy.

The more we make nature a priority in our lives, the more we understand that the mysterious divine force behind its creation intended us to find pleasure in nature—and to protect it from harm. ***Being in nature is being in heaven on earth.***

Where are your favorite places to explore and enjoy nature?

FAVORITE LOCAL PARKS:

LOCAL BEACHES, RIVERS, OR PONDS:

WOODS:

What time of day or week do you or could you set aside to spend in nature?

What are your favorite activities in nature? (examples: biking, walking, picnics, daydreaming)

What are some of the most spectacular nature scenes you have witnessed while traveling away from home?

What are some of the nature spots near your home on your wish list to visit?

What are some of the nature spots far from home on your wish list to visit?

Is there a particular wild animal(s) you feel a special connection to?

How do you keep reminders of nature's beauty in your home? (examples: buying fresh or dried flowers, keeping houseplants, collecting art with nature themes)

I support nature by . . . (examples: buying recycled products, donating money to nature or wildlife preserves, volunteering at a community garden, riding a bike, taking public transportation, carpooling, buying hybrid vehicles, supporting politicians who make preserving nature a priority)

How do you feel after you spend time in nature? (examples: calmer, closer to God, awestruck, energized)

Indoors, everything can be beautiful when we decorate our lives. Whether it's saving up to purchase a piece of handmade furniture that will one day be a family heirloom or getting a free hand-me-down dress from a friend, decorating our lives with beauty is like infusing each moment of our existence with a sacred blessing.

The perfect shade of lipstick. A sparkly bracelet on your wrist. An embroidered pillow on sale at your favorite store. Beauty doesn't have to be extravagant or expensive. It was not meant only for the few and the privileged. Rather, it is the universe's egalitarian desire that beauty be within everyone's grasp. ***No matter who you are, or how much money you have, your essence is light and love and beauty is your birthright here in heaven on earth.***

What are some of your favorite things in your home that make it beautiful?

CURTAINS, PILLOWS, THROWS, RUGS:

POTTERY, ART:

PLATES, SERVING DISHES, FURNITURE:

Which places in your home could use an infusion of beauty?

What decorations could you add to beautify your work space? (examples: plants, artwork, throw pillows, pretty picture frames)

What do you love about your appearance?

FAVORITE CLOTHES, JEWELRY, SHOES:

FAVORITE MAKEUP, HAIRSTYLE(S):

FAVORITE PHYSICAL FEATURES:

Which clothes, shoes, and such have you been meaning to update?

When was the last time you got a free makeover at the makeup counter?

What items do you need to update that you could find on sale?

What pretty purchases would be worth splurging on or investing in?

Which favorite heirlooms have been passed on to you?

Which pieces might you pass on as heirlooms to others?

Connoisseurs of beauty know the highest, purest form of beauty does not depend on outer appearances but resides within. Humility, compassion, joy—these are the ingredients for a stunning human being.

And the funny thing is, what's inside a person actually affects their outer appearance. Ever notice that the people you find most attractive are also kind, funny, or smart? Or have you noticed that when things are going well in your life, people often comment that you are "positively glowing"? That's because when people look at you, they are not just seeing your physical body—they are seeing your mind, your heart, your *soul*.

You can dress up rock stars in flashy shirts and tight pants, but they aren't irresistibly sexy until they've made a record that proves their talent, touches their fans, and stands the test of time. ***People who are contributing to heaven on earth are very attractive.***

What are some of your own favorite inner qualities? (examples: resilience, sense of humor, the wisdom that comes with age or experience)

What are some of your favorite inner qualities in a friend? (examples: good listener, considerate of others, fun-loving)

What are some of your favorite inner qualities in a mate? (examples: responsible, animal lover, music lover, sports lover, creative, passionate, affectionate, dreamer, traveler, community-minded, supportive)

Recall a time when you weren't initially drawn to someone, but after getting to know their personality, you found them extremely attractive.

Recall a time when you didn't think you would get along with someone based on their outer appearance, and after getting to know them, they became a treasured friend.

Name some of your own inner qualities that people have told you are attractive. (examples: your laugh, your passion for activism, your ability to nurture, your artistic talent, your sense of loyalty, your adventurous nature, your patience)

Name a celebrity who isn't considered traditionally attractive, or is perhaps only "cute" or "average" looking, but is now or has been in the past considered a sex symbol because of his or her personality or artistic ability. (examples: Mick Jagger, Jason Segel, Owen Wilson, Carly Simon, Maggie Gyllenhaal, Barbra Streisand)

HEART THOUGHTS

~to make beauty a central part of your daily life is to experience heaven on earth~

YOUR HEART THOUGHTS ON BEAUTY:

HEART THOUGHTS ON BEAUTY FROM YOUR FAVORITE MOVIES, BOOKS, AND SONGS:

HEART THOUGHTS ON BEAUTY FROM YOUR

FAMILY AND FRIENDS:

"If God were not willing
to forgive sin, heaven
would be empty."

- GERMAN PROVERB

CHAPTER 4

in heaven . . . you are forgiven

Forgiving ourselves becomes easier when we look at our lives through the eyes of Spirit. From a spiritual perspective, nothing is "unforgivable." Think about the most "unforgivable" thing you have ever done. Do you have a clear picture of it? Good. Here is God's response: "I love you unconditionally and will never abandon you. I know how much you regret hurting yourself and others. I'm so sorry for all the pain you have suffered because of this experience."

On a soul level you came to earth to learn and grow, to explore life and feel things deeply. That's an adventurous, messy, exciting, painful assignment. It's certainly not a simple one, so cut yourself some slack. After all, making mistakes and having regrets are part of God's plan, part of the learning, growing, exploring, and feeling you came here to do.

When you have trouble forgiving yourself, remember: Life is meant to be a journey of unconditional love, not an exercise in perfection or judgment. ***You had God's forgiveness instantly. Don't you think it's about time you forgave yourself? Heaven on earth demands it.***

Is there something you've done recently that you are having trouble forgiving yourself for? Does knowing that God forgives you make it any easier to forgive yourself?

Is there something you're having trouble forgiving yourself for that happened long ago? Something you have been carrying around with you for years? How might trying to begin forgiving yourself actually help the person or people or animals you hurt? (examples: A father might be more involved in his children's lives if he didn't feel so guilty around them, or a woman might give a loving home to a shelter dog if she could only forgive herself for unwittingly neglecting or injuring the pet she had as a child.)

Is there someone you would like forgiveness from, but the relationship is so strained that you are unlikely to receive it? Write a short note to that person here, explaining how much you regret hurting them and how you have suffered because of it. Reread the note, and let the remorse and pain in your words inspire you to forgive yourself.

Is there someone you would like forgiveness from, but they have passed on? Write them a short, sincere note here, asking for their forgiveness. Then watch for signs from heaven that they heard you and your wish has been granted.

Was there a time when you forgave yourself for something that seemed unforgivable? How did you feel before and after getting your own forgiveness?

If you are having trouble forgiving yourself, ask for help from Spirit. Write a short note here asking God to help you release the pain of judgment and replace it with love. Also record any dreams, feelings, and synchronicities about this situation that might be signs from Spirit.

How easy is it for you to forgive yourself for small, everyday things? The better you get at absolving yourself of these minor infractions, the easier it will get for you to love yourself through the bigger ones. Is there something small that you could forgive yourself for right now?

Were your parents or guardians good at forgiving you? Were they able to forgive themselves? Or were they judgmental and unyielding?

Think back to a time in the distant past when you needed forgiveness and a little extra nurturing. See that younger version of yourself, in the middle of a crisis, desperately wanting self-love and forgiveness. Go ahead and imagine giving that younger version of you a big, comforting hug. Record your feelings here.

Forgiving others means accepting who they are, and where they are in their life's journey. A partner with narcissistic tendencies might be incapable of expressing empathy. A mother with rage issues might be incapable of always keeping her anger in check, especially if she has yet to realize she needs professional help. A boss or teacher who is dealing with a personal crisis may be incapable of acting as an attentive mentor on the job, at least while that person's home life is in chaos. When we examine not only the upsetting situation but also the people involved, it becomes easier to forgive the folks who have caused us pain.

Everyone's emotional and psychological makeup is different. Everyone has different life circumstances and different methods of coping with trauma, stress, and the expectations of others. Most people are doing the best they can at any given point in time. And most people don't walk out the door in the morning intending to wound or alienate anyone. When we see people for who they are, not who we wish they were, it's easier to forgive their actions and develop a greater compassion for all of humanity.

Having a context of who someone is when they hurt you doesn't make the pain go away, but it can help you understand the real motivation behind their actions—and that can most certainly make your pain significantly less. ***Heaven on earth is understanding others so we can forgive them.***

Is there someone you forgave because their life or emotional circumstances helped explain their words or behavior?

___

___

___

Get quiet and ask your higher self who you are currently having the most trouble forgiving. Now ask your higher self what are the circumstances in that person's life that might help you soften toward them or at least be able to forgive them and then move on from your relationship with this person. Record the answers you receive here.

___

___

___

___

Think of a time in your life when you did something you regret and hurt someone else in the process. What were the circumstances around that event that might help explain your actions or words?

Sometimes the easiest way to forgive someone is to picture the person as a young child: innocent, trusting, and full of love. That young child is still inside every adult, despite the pain, disappointment, cruelty, judgment, fear, and abandonment they may have encountered in their life's journey. Picture as a young child someone you are having trouble forgiving right now and hold the image of that person in your mind and heart for a few minutes. Did this affect your feelings toward him or her? Your ability to forgive?

Can you recall a time when someone forgave you even though they might have had cause to hold a grudge?

HOW DID THEIR FORGIVENESS MAKE YOU FEEL?

People often say that forgiving someone is a gift you give to yourself, because it can help you move past the pain you may be holding on to and heal. But forgiveness can also be an enormous blessing to the person you choose to forgive. Is there someone in your life that you could forgive that might see your forgiveness as a precious, healing event?

Is there someone you have not forgiven who, if they passed away suddenly, you would regret not making peace with?

If you were on your deathbed, coming to the end of your life here on earth, are there any people you would want to forgive? If any names come to mind, forgive them now.

Forgiving people can take many forms: in person, through a letter, during a phone call, in an email, or via text. And remember, just because you forgive someone doesn't mean you want them in your life (something perhaps best expressed through a letter or email). How have you forgiven people in the past?

We don't have to allow someone to be part of our lives in order to forgive them. Is there someone like this in your life?

HOW DID IT FEEL AFTER YOU FORGAVE THEM? WAS IT HELPFUL OR HEALING TO YOU IN ANY WAY?

What happens when you can't forgive someone? It's important to honor your feelings and be honest with yourself when you can't forgive someone for the harm they caused you or someone you love. Usually this happens when the wound is very deep and the pain you felt was, at the time of the incident, overwhelming. The anger you have toward this person probably waxes and wanes but never fully goes away.

When we can't forgive someone, we can work instead on acceptance—accepting what they said or did, accepting that it cannot be changed, accepting your pain, and even accepting that, at least right now, you cannot forgive them. Sometimes not forgiving someone is our battle with reality. We are unable to come to terms with the injustice or hurt we suffered—almost unable to believe it actually happened. Not forgiving someone could also be our way of hanging onto our pain, which can feel familiar or even soothing. Perhaps you will just never be able to forgive this person. That's okay. But if this is the case, it's important to work with acceptance. Forgiveness helps the person who was hurt to move on, to begin healing, or to experience a whole new level of healing. ***Acceptance will also enable you to move on, to heal and to find heaven on earth once more.***

Is there a person, or people, in your life that you have tried to forgive but can't, at least not right now?

Describe how they hurt you, expressing exactly how their words or actions made you feel.

Describe your anger toward the people who hurt you.

How often do you think about the person or people who hurt you?

How often do you think about what they did or said that you just can't seem to forgive?

Do you feel your anger toward this person or people has held you back in your life? Has it stopped you from fully experiencing joy or love or friendship or peace of mind or career opportunities?

If you could say anything to this person or people about the rage or sadness you feel, what would it be? Please write them a note here.

TAKE A MOMENT AND READ THE NOTE YOU WROTE TO THE PERSON OR PEOPLE YOU CANNOT FORGIVE. SIT WITH THOSE WORDS FOR A MOMENT, AND LET THEM FILL YOU WITH COMPASSION FOR YOURSELF, FOR ALL YOU HAVE SUFFERED. GIVE YOURSELF A HUG, TELL YOURSELF "I LOVE YOU" IN THE MIRROR, OR DO SOME OTHER SPECIAL THING TO COMFORT YOURSELF. HOW DO YOU FEEL?

How does it make you feel to know that whatever happened that has wounded you cannot be taken back or changed? (examples: mad, peaceful, numb, shocked, sad, reflective)

Whatever happened cannot be changed or taken back, but it is also in the past. It's over, and you don't have to relive it every day. How does that make you feel? (examples: relieved, angry, scared, free, happy)

How have you, or might you, seek out healing for this wound? (examples: books, therapy, medical doctors, massage, meditation, exercise, volunteering, support from loved ones, spiritual support)

Have you shared this wound with the people closest to you whom you trust?

As a symbol of your willingness to work on acceptance, perform a ceremony where you acknowledge that what happened cannot be changed or altered and that you want to release this person's hold on you and your life. (examples: writing down the name of the person you can't forgive and then ripping up the piece of paper and throwing it in the trash or going to your favorite spot in nature and asking God to help release you from thoughts about this person)

HEART THOUGHTS

~heaven on earth is forgiving yourself, forgiving others, and accepting what cannot be changed~

YOUR HEART THOUGHTS ABOUT FORGIVENESS:

HEART THOUGHTS ABOUT FORGIVENESS FROM YOUR FAVORITE MOVIES, BOOKS, AND SONGS:

HEART THOUGHTS ABOUT FORGIVENESS FROM YOUR FRIENDS AND FAMILY:

"The connections we make in the course of a life—maybe that's what heaven is."

- FRED ROGERS,
HOST OF *MISTER ROGER'S NEIGHBORHOOD*

CHAPTER 5

in heaven . . . you are your best self

Often when people have near-death experiences, they describe visiting a place similar to heaven, where they feel like the best versions of themselves. Could you feel this way on earth today? The answer depends upon the current level of self-care in your life.

Self-care is a concept I learned about from bestselling author and life coach Cheryl Richardson in her book *The Art of Extreme Self-Care*. Self-care means being good stewards of our physical, emotional, spiritual, and financial health. Good self-care allows us a high quality of life right here, right now.

So many people place their own needs and wants last on their to-do list. They are more focused on being providers and caregivers for others. But no one who is tired, unhappy, and stressed can truly be there for someone else. That's why taking exceptional care of yourself is the most selfless act you can perform. Taking good care of yourself gives you the best life possible—and allows you to give more to those you love and the world around you. ***Heaven on earth is about caring for yourself as much as you care for others.***

How do you take care of yourself physically?

WHAT IS YOUR FAVORITE WAY TO EXERCISE?

WHAT SUPPLEMENTS DO YOU TAKE DAILY?

WHAT DOCTORS DO YOU SEE ANNUALLY OR REGULARLY?

WHAT MEDICAL CONDITION(S) ARE YOU CURRENTLY MANAGING?

WHO OR WHAT HELPS SUPPORT YOU IN MANAGING THESE CONDITIONS? (EXAMPLES: DOCTORS, THERAPISTS, SUPPORT GROUPS, LOVED ONES)

___

___

___

___

___

___

Who can you talk to for emotional support?

THERAPIST OR HEALTH-CARE PROFESSIONAL:

___

___

___

___

___

___

FRIENDS:

FAMILY MEMBERS:

COWORKERS:

What are your favorite ways to relax when you feel stressed?

How do you nurture yourself when you are hurt or afraid?

How do you pump yourself up or get your fire and hope back when you are discouraged?

Do you make it a priority to explore, process, and learn from your emotions, even the negative ones?

Do you schedule regular "me" time once a day, even if it's brief? Do you have extended "me" time at least once a week?

WHAT ARE YOUR FAVORITE WAYS TO RECHARGE OR UNWIND DURING "ME" TIME?

How do you take care of yourself spiritually?

WHAT RELIGIONS OR SPIRITUAL PHILOSOPHIES RESONATE WITH YOU?

WHO ARE YOUR FAVORITE SPIRITUAL AUTHORS, AND WHAT ARE YOUR FAVORITE SPIRITUAL TEXTS?

WHICH SPIRITUAL LEADERS, PAST AND PRESENT, INSPIRE YOU?

DO YOU PRACTICE SPIRITUAL RITUALS, CEREMONIES, OR MEDITATIONS ON A REGULAR BASIS?

ARE YOU A MEMBER OF ANY CHURCHES OR OTHER SPIRITUAL COMMUNITIES?

ARE YOUR FRIENDS AND FAMILY MEMBERS SUPPORTIVE OF YOUR SPIRITUAL BELIEFS?

How do you take care of yourself financially?

DO YOU WORK OUTSIDE THE HOME?

HOW DO YOU PLAN FOR YOUR FINANCIAL FUTURE, AND WHAT ARE YOUR FINANCIAL GOALS?

WHAT ACTION STEPS (SMALL ONES COUNT) ARE YOU TAKING, OR COULD YOU TAKE, TOWARD YOUR FINANCIAL GOALS?

DO YOU HAVE A REGULAR SAVINGS PLAN, EVEN IF IT IS ONLY A SMALL AMOUNT EVERY MONTH?

DO YOU AND YOUR IMMEDIATE FAMILY ADHERE TO A BUDGET?

What are you struggling with most right now in your life?

DO YOU HAVE ANY FRIENDS OR ACQUAINTANCES WHO HAVE BEEN THROUGH A SIMILAR SITUATION THAT YOU COULD SPEAK TO?

ARE THERE ANY BOOKS BY EXPERTS ON THIS SUBJECT THAT YOU COULD READ, SUPPORT GROUPS YOU COULD JOIN, OR PROFESSIONALS IN THIS FIELD YOU COULD SPEAK TO?

Being your best self means being of service to others. Serving others is the most noble and rewarding manifestation of our heart's energy—and our soul's ultimate purpose on earth. How well we serve others is the litmus test for success in all of our relationships and roles in society.

When people say they are searching for meaning in their lives, they are really searching for a way to be of service.

After taking good care of ourselves, our next priority is to take good care of others. Serving can be as obvious as donating a large amount of money or time to a charity or as subtle as offering to make dinner when you see that your partner has had a long day. ***Heaven on earth for everyone depends upon each individual being of service to others.***

How are you of service each day to your immediate family?

WHAT ARE SOME WAYS YOU MIGHT BETTER SERVE THEM?

How are you of service to close friends and coworkers?

WHAT ARE SOME WAYS YOU MIGHT BETTER SERVE THEM?

How are you serving others through your job?

HOW MIGHT YOU BETTER SERVE OTHERS THROUGH YOUR WORK?

How are you serving your community?

How can you contribute to healing the planet?

Are you now, or have you ever been, a volunteer?

IF SO, WHAT DID YOU LEARN FROM YOUR VOLUNTEER EXPERIENCE, AND HOW DID YOU GROW FROM THOSE LESSONS? IF NOT, WHAT TYPE OF VOLUNTEER WORK MIGHT INTEREST YOU?

How does serving others make you feel?
(examples: needed, fulfilled, grateful, humble)

Existing on this planet is not about just being alive, but *feeling* alive. What are your passions? What could you spend hours doing and still lose track of time? What would you do with your days if you had all the money you needed? What do you wish you could change about the world? What gets you excited? What makes you feel grateful to simply be alive?

Passion makes existence more than just joyful. Passion makes existence *thrilling*. A life without passion is two dimensional—with passion we achieve depth and wholeness. If you are regularly bored or lethargic, you have probably lost touch with your passions.

When our passions are part of our daily existence we feel alive, we are our best selves, and we experience the thrill of heaven on earth.

What are your favorite hobbies?

____

____

____

What are your favorite movies?

What are your favorite books?

What are your favorite musical acts?

What subject(s) would you like to learn more about?

What was the last workshop or event you attended that significantly contributed to your personal growth?

What do you want to change about the world?

What social or political causes are close to your heart?

What would you like to accomplish before you die?

What parts of the world have you always wanted to visit?

What activities make you feel most grateful to be alive?

What activity makes you lose all track of time?

What would you do if you had all the money you needed?

What would you do if your family and friends supported your choice unconditionally?

What kinds of events on your calendar do you most look forward to? (examples: pitching a new idea to your boss, meeting with potential clients, concerts, out-of-town trips, dates to hang out with friends, attending sporting events, going to readings or Q&As with your favorite writers and artists, volunteering or activist events, spiritual retreats, family time)

HEAVEN IS WHERE THE HEART IS

HEART THOUGHTS

~heaven on earth is taking good care of everyone we love, especially ourselves~

YOUR HEART THOUGHTS ABOUT

BEING YOUR BEST SELF:

HEART THOUGHTS ABOUT BEING YOUR BEST SELF FROM YOUR FAVORITE MOVIES, BOOKS, OR SONGS:

HEART THOUGHTS ABOUT BEING YOUR BEST SELF FROM YOUR FRIENDS AND FAMILY:

“For he shall give his angels
charge over thee, to keep
thee in all thy ways.”

— PSALMS 91:11

CHAPTER 6

in heaven . . . angels watch over you

Angels don't always wear wings and halos. Often they look like businesspeople or students or even small children. If you want proof of the existence of angels, observe the tiny angelic actions of humans who make up everyday life.

Angels can look like the stranger who smiles and holds the elevator so you can squeeze in at the last moment. Or they can look like the woman who pets and comforts a dog nervously waiting for his owner to come out of a store—or the man who pays for the groceries of the woman in line in front of him after her credit card is declined. This life can be overflowing with anonymous acts of kindness.

These tiny angelic actions make up a very small part of your day, but they are often the most memorable at the end of it. ***Heaven on earth is a mosaic of tiny angelic moments.***

When was the last time a stranger acted as an angel in your life?

When was the most memorable time a stranger acted as an angel in your life?

Is there a remarkable story you read in the news or heard from a friend about a stranger acting as an angel?

When was the last time you acted angelically toward someone you didn't know?

When was the most memorable time you acted as an angel in a stranger's life?

Describe an extraordinary act of angelic kindness between strangers that you personally witnessed.

Are there any small ways that you could be an angel to strangers you encounter every day?

IN YOUR NEIGHBORHOOD:

IN YOUR OFFICE BUILDING:

ON THE WAY TO AND FROM WORK:

IN STORES:

TO PEOPLE WHO ARE PERFORMING A SERVICE FOR YOU:

Have you ever prayed for a stranger? Pick someone out of the crowd: a homeless person, a disgruntled cashier, a stressed-out mom in the grocery store. Then spend a few moments sending that person light and love. Throughout the week, whenever it pops into your head, picture the stranger and pray for him or her again. The following week start over with someone new. This exercise will help open your heart and increase your capacity for empathy. How does praying for a stranger make you feel?

DESCRIBE STRANGERS YOU HAVE PRAYED FOR IN THE PAST.

While we love to be reminded of the angelic nature of humans in small everyday ways, it's even more inspiring to know that mere mortals can act angelically in our lives in extraordinary ways, for example, the health-care professionals who offer guidance and support after a terrifying diagnosis, the friend who holds your hand through a divorce, the mentor who gives you your big career break, or the family member who offers you a free place to stay so you can afford to go back to school.

Along with the winged celestial entities whose lives are devoted to watching over us, humans who perform extraordinary acts of kindness and support are also guardian angels. They guard over us—and heaven on earth.

Who are the people in your life you consider guardian angels, and how did, or do they, support you?

FAMILY MEMBERS:

____

____

____

FRIENDS:

COWORKERS:

HEALTH-CARE PROFESSIONALS:

HOW DID YOU OR DO YOU TELL THEM THANK YOU?

Has someone ever inspired you, just by their actions in their own life, to accomplish something big, such as start a family, buy a house, change careers, stand up for yourself, leave a toxic relationship, or face an illness? Have you ever told them in person or on paper how much the example they set meant to you?

When have you put on a set of wings for a friend, family member, or coworker?

HOW DID IT MAKE YOU FEEL WHEN YOU HELPED THEM?

Is there someone in your life who is struggling right now whom you might help in an extraordinary way?

When have you felt the comforting presence of a friend or family member's support after that person has passed on?

WHAT SIGNS HAVE YOU RECEIVED THAT LET YOU KNOW THAT DECEASED FRIENDS AND FAMILY MEMBERS ARE STILL WATCHING OUT FOR YOU AS GUARDIAN ANGELS FROM HEAVEN?

Is there something you're struggling with right now? If so, use this space to describe your problem, and ask God to send a human guardian angel to aid you.

Besides the billions of human angels on our planet, there are also divine creatures whose task is to guide and protect every human life. You might sense their presence whenever a feeling of peace permeates your soul, when you notice a stray white feather in your path, or when a voice whispers words of comfort or encouragement in your ear. Or you might even catch a glimpse of one: their majestic wings, noble expression, and powerful energy. All these signs are evidence of angels at work in your life.

Whenever your world has been blessed by grace, unconditional love, or healing, you can be certain it has been blessed by an angel. Angels come from heaven, but they love to visit heaven on earth.

When have you experienced love or grace or healing that made you suspect an angel's presence in your life?

What signs have you received of an angel's presence?

What guidance have you received from your angels?

How have you been contacted by angels in the past? (examples: in dreams, in visions, hearing angelic voices, sensing during a challenging time that you were not alone, experiencing divine coincidences, feeling a sudden strength or calmness during a time of fear or crisis)

What are your favorite books, movies, or songs about angels?

What is your favorite angel story, either one you've read about in the news, read in a sacred text, or heard from someone you know?

Do you keep reminders of angels around your home or office?

Feel closer to your guardian angel by learning your angel's name. Become silent, and ask your higher self for your guardian angel's name. Often your higher self or your angel will answer by placing the name in your mind. Or, give your guardian angel a name that makes you feel cherished and protected every time you think of it. Don't be surprised if more than one name is whispered in your ear, as we all have several guardian angels (and other angels who come and go throughout our life, depending on our circumstances and needs). Some angels have regal names, like Celestia, while other names might be more practical, like the name of one of my guardian angels, Sharon. You can do this exercise for every member of your family, because every person has guardian angels assigned to them at birth. Write down the names of your guardian angels.

WHAT ARE SOME NAMES OF GUARDIAN ANGELS WHO WATCH OVER FRIENDS OR FAMILY MEMBERS?

One of the easiest ways to experience angelic healing is to pray for angels to change your energy or mood. If you are intensely angry or scared long after the emotion should have run its course, an angel can lift that emotion from you instantly and replace it with peace or even joy. Try asking an angel to change your energy the next time you can't seem to let go of a negative emotion. Record the experience here.

Have you ever seen an angel? If so, describe the experience. If not, what do you imagine the experience would be like?

DESCRIBE THE PHYSICAL APPEARANCE OF THE ANGEL YOU SAW. SOMETIMES ANGELS WILL SHOW THEMSELVES TO YOU IN THEIR NATURAL DIVINE STATE—FEATHERY WINGS, FLOWING WHITE ROBES—AND OTHER TIMES THEY WILL ASSUME A HUMAN FORM. IF YOU'VE NEVER SEEN AN ANGEL, HOW DO YOU LIKE TO IMAGINE ONE IN YOUR MIND'S EYE?

WHAT WAS GOING ON IN YOUR LIFE WHEN YOUR ANGEL APPEARED TO YOU? OFTEN ANGELS WILL SHOW THEMSELVES AT PIVOTAL MOMENTS IN OUR SOUL'S JOURNEY ON EARTH.

WHAT FEELING DID YOU GET FROM SEEING YOUR ANGEL? COMFORT? CONFIDENCE? STRENGTH? (DON'T BE ALARMED IF SEEING AN ANGEL FEELS SCARY. THIS IS A COMMON INITIAL REACTION—I WAS TERRIFIED WHEN I SAW AN ANGEL. BUT ONCE THE SHOCK WORE OFF, IT BECAME ONE OF MY MOST TREASURED MEMORIES.) IF YOU HAVE NEVER SEEN AN ANGEL, HOW DO YOU THINK YOU WOULD REACT IF YOU DID SEE ONE?

HEAVEN IS WHERE THE HEART IS

HEART THOUGHTS

~heaven on earth is
populated by angels—
both celestial and human~

YOUR HEART THOUGHTS ABOUT ANGELS:

HEART THOUGHTS ABOUT ANGELS FROM YOUR FAVORITE MOVIES, BOOKS, OR SONGS:

HEART THOUGHTS ABOUT ANGELS FROM YOUR FRIENDS AND FAMILY:

"Heaven means to be
one with God."

—CONFUCIUS

CHAPTER 7

in heaven . . . peace is with you

Our hearts can be in a constant state of changing, extreme emotions, many of which are rooted in desire or fear. You are scared your boss is unhappy with your performance. You want the boy who sits behind you in class to think you're pretty. You're terrified about your friend's operation. You pray every night that you can scrape together a down payment for a house. How can we cultivate a divine sense of peace in a world full of such earthly yearning and pain?

Take two steps back from desire and fear, and shift your heart's focus toward gratitude. Instead of worrying (for the tenth time in twenty-four hours) about whether or not your son will pass math this semester, take two steps back from this situation, and shift your focus toward gratitude by admiring the sunset from your front porch. Instead of obsessing about the test results you'll receive from your doctor tomorrow morning, take two steps back from this situation, and shift your focus toward gratitude by savoring time with your family around the dinner table.

It is one of the hard-and-fast rules of the universe, as trustworthy as any law of physics: Gratitude brings peace and unlocks the gates to the kingdom of heaven on earth.

Is there a situation in your life that you need to take two steps back from to gain more peace?

Can you remember a time when you put space between yourself and an upsetting situation and this break actually helped you better handle or resolve the situation?

What are some of your favorite healthy distractions when you need to take your mind off something upsetting?

What are some of the things you are most grateful for in your life right now?

WITH FAMILY/FRIENDS:

WITH YOUR HEALTH:

WITH RELATIONSHIPS:

AT YOUR JOB OR IN YOUR CAREER:

IN THE WORLD:

What are some of the things you should be grateful for but probably take for granted?

Recall a time when you wanted something desperately and years later were glad you didn't get it.

Recall a time when you wanted something desperately, but when you got it, you realized it was nothing like what you expected or wanted.

Name a place where you can go to feel more peaceful.

Which people in your life make you feel most peaceful?

Which movies, books, or songs make you feel peaceful?

Is everything basically okay right now in your life, at this specific moment in time? Even if you are facing great challenges, the odds are that you have what you need to face them or have an idea about how to get what you need. List several ways that things are basically okay right now in your life. (examples: food, shelter, employment, loved ones, health, access to good doctors and medication)

Recall a time when you were terrified of something and it never happened:

Recall a time when you were terrified of something, and the fear you felt anticipating the event was far worse than the event itself:

There are times when events in our lives make peace of mind seem impossible. The person you love no longer loves you back. The career you counted on and spent years working toward is over. An injury changes your body forever. In these cases our instinct is often to fight, to reject our current reality. Yet perhaps the heart's only path to peace is via surrender. Once we surrender to a set of circumstances that we cannot change, we begin to find peace. But when we surrender, something else happens too: the universe is able to offer us aid and unexpected blessings.

When we are in crisis, life can feel like walking a tightrope; yet underneath that tightrope is an enormous, invisible net. We don't have to walk through a crisis like we're on a dangerous, narrow path. We can relax and fall into the grace and comfort that is all around. Once we stop fighting reality and surrender to it, we can focus our energy on recognizing and using the opportunities and resources the universe *always* provides, such as the friend who went through a similar situation and offers you priceless advice and empathy, or the health-care professional who acts as a guide through your healing process, or a family member who has an open position in their business you can fill.

When we surrender to circumstances beyond our control, we not only find peace—the universe also works magic in our lives. The kind of magic that reveals heaven on earth.

Name a time when you found peace by surrendering to circumstances that were beyond your control.

DESCRIBE HOW YOU FELT EMOTIONALLY BEFORE YOU SURRENDERED AND AFTER.

Name a time when you were able to relax during a crisis and this peaceful state helped you see the situation with new eyes and an open mind.

Name a time when the universe worked magic in your life when you were in crisis.

WHAT ARE SOME OF THE SPECIFIC BLESSINGS THAT HAPPENED DURING THIS TIME?

Name a time when the universe worked magic in the life of a friend or family member when they were in crisis.

Is there a situation in your life right now that you need to surrender to?

NAME SOME OF THE OBVIOUS, IMMEDIATE BENEFITS OF SURRENDERING TO THIS SITUATION. (EXAMPLES: INSTEAD OF USING YOUR ENERGY TO FIGHT THE SITUATION YOU CAN USE IT TO HEAL OR MOVE ON, INSTEAD OF CLINGING TO THE PAST YOU CAN START PLANNING FOR THE FUTURE)

Is there a situation in the life of a close friend or family member that would benefit from surrender?

When your heart is disappointed, discouraged, or confused, have faith. Remind yourself that perhaps whatever discomfort you are experiencing at this moment will be for the greater good later. Some events can only be fully understood in hindsight. Until then, have faith.

Possibly a romantic relationship is ending because its main purpose was to teach you a lesson that will prepare you to meet your soul mate. Maybe the physical or emotional challenges you were born with have made you more sensitive to the pain of others and enabled you to become a gifted healer.

Faith helps our hearts find peace by reminding us that challenging circumstances might be an important part of our spiritual journey here in heaven on earth.

When has a situation that at first appeared negative turned out to be a blessing in disguise?

Have you experienced a situation that seemed senseless at the time yet made perfect sense in hindsight?

What are some of the challenges you have faced in life that might have added to your character or enabled you to help others?

When have you had a relationship that helped prepare you for a more significant relationship later on?

When have you had a career failure that taught you a valuable lesson that later led to success?

When has a loved one given you criticism that was painful to hear at the time but that you greatly benefited from later?

When has a boss or coworker given you criticism that was painful to hear at the time but that you greatly benefited from later?

Are there any challenges you have faced that you feel your soul was meant to experience?

How has Spirit made its presence known to you when you were in crisis?

Have you ever experienced a crisis that deepened your faith or brought you closer to God? How so?

Explain the word "faith" using your own experiences to define the term.

HEART THOUGHTS

~heaven on earth means choosing peace~

YOUR HEART THOUGHTS ON PEACE:

HEART THOUGHTS ON PEACE FROM YOUR FAVORITE MOVIES, BOOKS, OR SONGS:

HEART THOUGHTS ON PEACE FROM YOUR

FRIENDS AND FAMILY:

"The experience of eternity
right here and now is the
function of life. Heaven is not
the place to have the experience;
here is the place to have
the experience."

- JOSEPH CAMPBELL

CHAPTER 8

in heaven . . . your heart is free

Your heart is free when it's lost in the moment, untethered by the worries or anticipations of day-to-day living. I feel lost in the moment when I am riding my bike along the majestic Hudson River, when I hold my husband's hand and sense that I am deeply loved and treasured, when I am so absorbed in a writing project that I lose track of time, when I am moved to tears by one of my favorite songs, when I laugh long and loud with a friend, when I am surrounded by silence and trees, when I hold my rose-quartz heart stone and pray, when I feel God's presence in a spiritual space.

Freedom is escaping the temporary cares of this world and connecting with the eternal. ***What is eternal in this life is that which is constant, that which speaks to our soul: the love of a close friend or family member, God's presence in our lives, the wonder and beauty of nature. It's the thrill of pursuing your life's work. It's the ability of art to touch us and change us. It's the simple joy of laughter, the holy quality of silence, and the comfort of prayer. It's heaven on earth.***

What activities make you feel lost in the moment?

What places make you feel lost in the moment?

Which people make you feel lost in the moment?

Are there some people in your life who are very good at living in the moment?

Was there a time in your life when you were better at living in the moment?

WHAT WAS DIFFERENT ABOUT YOUR LIFE THEN?

HOW OR WHY DID THIS CHANGE?

Which activities or places or people make you feel connected to the eternal?

Is there a spot in nature near your home that speaks to your soul?

Did you ever go on vacation and find a spot in nature that spoke to your soul?

Which relationships in your life resonate with you on a soul level? (examples: you feel a strong connection to someone, you clicked with them immediately, they "get" you, you feel as if they have always been part of your life, you sense that God sent them into your life at just the right time, it's hard to imagine your life without them, they have been great teachers and contributed to your personal growth and/or you contributed to theirs)

____

____

____

____

What do you feel is your life's work? Or what contribution(s) did your soul come here to make? (examples: being a mother, being a wife, working as a scientist, working as a teacher, being a healer, helping others whenever you can, spreading joy, spreading love, making music, being an activist)

____

____

____

Where do you go to feel God's presence?

Do you have a favorite prayer or spiritual song that touches your soul?

Is laughter a part of your daily life?

What words would you use to define that which is eternal in this life? (examples: love, joy, beauty, hope, faith, birth, Spirit)

We can feel freer in our outer reality through our inner reality. How do you picture yourself in your mind's eye? I'm not talking about seeing yourself scramble through an overdue project at work, or stand in line at the grocery store, or negotiate a curfew with your teenager. I'm talking about how you picture your *soul.*

A rock band from the 1970s made a documentary where each member of the group filmed a "fantasy sequence." The lead singer arranged footage of himself galloping on a stallion through breathtaking Welsh countryside, finding a sacred sword, and rescuing a princess held hostage in a castle. The guitarist shot his sequence at midnight beneath a full moon in the dramatic Scottish Highlands. As he scaled a mountain, a hermit waited at the top, ready to bestow upon him profound mystical knowledge. Meanwhile, the drummer simply had a film crew take footage of him doing the things he loved best: dancing around the house with his wife, teaching his son to play the drums, and driving his favorite motorcycle.

When I want to feel free, sometimes I picture myself in the ornate robes of an ancient priestess or as a Native American warrior fighting for the conservation of our planet. And other times I just picture myself getting a massage at my local spa or acting silly with my husband on a lazy Saturday afternoon. I call these my freedom mental images. ***We all need freedom mental images as reminders of our soul's magnificent and playful nature. And as reminders that life can be heaven on earth.***

What are some of your current freedom mental images (or how do you picture yourself in your daydreams)?

____

____

____

____

____

WHAT DO THESE IMAGES REVEAL ABOUT YOU?

____

____

____

____

What do you have the most fun doing?

Who are the people you have the most fun with?

What are some of your past freedom mental images?

If you could be any person from history, who would it be and why?

How do you feel when you concentrate on your freedom mental image?

How could you incorporate more of your freedom mental images into your daily reality?

Do you ever dress or act like the images or characters from your daydreams?

IF YOU DO, DO YOU FEEL FREER? HOW ELSE DO YOU FEEL? IF NOT, IMAGINE HOW YOU MIGHT FEEL IF YOU DID SO.

In my late thirties I had a midlife crisis. It reminded me of childhood when I first realized I was going to die one day. I was so terrified I was paralyzed. "It's all I think about," my six-year-old self confessed to my mother.

"Well," she said, "that's a good way to waste your life. If you're going to spend your time thinking about how you'll die someday, you might as well be dead already." Her advice was perfect—then. But once I hit my late thirties I found myself needing to revisit the notion that I would one day die. Only this time I didn't find the idea terrifying; I found it incredibly liberating. Suddenly I wanted to squeeze pleasure and meaning out of every moment.

The best revelation I had was about freedom. Why was I so worried about everything? I had roughly eighty years on the planet, if I was lucky, and then I'd be gone. Why couldn't I let go of mistakes I'd made in the past, and why did I talk myself out of adventures I longed to go on in the future? That way of thinking didn't make me feel free; it made me feel trapped. And my time on this planet is too precious to spend in prison.

Freedom is realizing that your time on this planet is limited. ***This means that every day is precious, every day is sacred, every day is an adventure. And every day deserves to be heaven on earth.***

Is there a once-in-a-lifetime adventure you are longing to go on in the near future?

What once-in-a-lifetime adventures have you already been on?

What do you want to be remembered for when you are dead?

REMEMBERED BY YOUR FAMILY AND FRIENDS FOR:

REMEMBERED BY SOCIETY, CLIENTS, AND COWORKERS FOR:

Is there something you will regret if you don't do it before you die?

Is there someone you need to forgive or make peace with before you die?

Do you have a "bucket list," and if so, what are some of the top entries on it?

What are some of the mistakes you beat yourself up for that, in the grand scheme of life, aren't really that terrible?

Are there things you worry about on a regular basis that, in the grand scheme of life, aren't really that important?

HEAVEN IS WHERE THE HEART IS

HEART THOUGHTS

~heaven on earth is realizing that your heart always was, and always will be, free~

YOUR HEART THOUGHTS ABOUT FREEDOM:

HEART THOUGHTS ABOUT FREEDOM FROM YOUR FAVORITE MOVIES, BOOKS, AND SONGS:

HEART THOUGHTS ABOUT FREEDOM FROM

YOUR FRIENDS AND FAMILY:

conclusion

The idea for this journal first came to me several years ago. I jotted down notes, but when it was time to actually do some real writing, I struggled. I knew the idea for the book was good, but as I reread my thoughts about creating heaven on earth they didn't resonate with me. Reluctantly I printed out all my notes for the book, stuck them in a folder, and literally put this project on the shelf.

About a year later, I was chatting with a friend during coffee hour after church. He is also a writer and was working on his second book. Not only had his first book been a commercial success, but I also really enjoyed reading it. "How is the new book coming?" I asked.

"It's . . . coming," he said. We both laughed because he'd been working on this book for quite a while now—long enough that I expected his answer to be, "my agent and I are shopping it to publishers" or "my editor loves the first three chapters."

"I'm sorry," I said. "I don't mean to pressure you. I'm just curious about when I can read it because I loved your first book."

He sighed and shook his head like he was about to impart one of life's hard truths. "You know, Tanya, I realized something writing my first book: If *you* don't learn anything while you're writing it, no one else will learn from it either."

He paused for dramatic emphasis, and I nodded my head like I was "getting it," although I really didn't understand.

"So writing a book can't be rushed," he continued, throwing up his hands. "These things happen on their own timetable."

I finished my tea and walked out into the sunshine in the church courtyard. *Writer's block*, I thought on my way home, recalling my conversation with my friend. *It's funny the excuses we make when we are just stuck or nervous about showing other people our work.*

Another year passed, and eventually I leafed through that folder where I'd shelved all my ideas about a book for creating heaven on earth. *I'd do this completely differently now*, I thought as I looked over my notes. I sat down at my computer, and this journal poured out. I loved the words I was writing. I was challenged, surprised, and intrigued by the ideas coming out. Everything was gelling and flowing. Everything was different than the first time I'd tried to write this book, because my friend was right. This time I was learning something. That's because I finally had something to *teach*.

During those two years while I didn't work on this book, I was undergoing some important personal growth.

I remember realizing one random afternoon that I didn't consciously try to seek out happiness each day. I asked a few friends, and they agreed that proactively going after happiness wasn't something in the front of their minds every day either. I started exploring what made me happy: beautiful things, spending time in nature, developing strong connections with people, feeling free, finding peace in whatever challenges life threw me, nurturing myself, being quicker to forgive myself, helping others—all the things that would inspire each chapter of this book. I basically spent two years researching this book, although because I'd put the idea for a book about heaven on earth out of my mind, I didn't even realize I was doing research!

My friend was right about many things. The most important projects happen on their own timetable, such as buying a house, starting a family, falling in love, finding your dream job—or creating your own heaven on earth. So don't be discouraged if you read this book and your life doesn't suddenly transform into heaven on earth (although I bet that as you work with this journal your life will instantly become more heavenly). Let the words and ideas here—mine and yours—steep in your soul. If heaven on earth is something you want, something you consciously and proactively go after—you'll get there. And eventually living there every day will become second nature. You most certainly deserve heaven on earth, and it is most definitely attainable.

Acknowledgments

The author wishes to thank the following people for their help and support during the writing of this book: Linda Konner, Kate Zimmermann, Edward Grinnan, Colleen Hughes, Walker Lamond, Jess Richardson, Charles Richardson, Doug Snyder, Keren Baltzer, Cathryn Zommer, Laura Langlie, Amy Tietjen, Kate Crane, Jana Carroll, JD Carroll and family (Kristen Carroll, Paulette, and Mike), Michael Biamonte, Doug Willen, Danielle Desimone-Koester, Aileen Blitz, and my husband.

About the Author

Tanya Richardson is an editor for the inspirational publisher Guideposts, founded by *Power of Positive Thinking* author Norman Vincent Peale. Tanya contributes regularly to *Angels on Earth* magazine, where she ghostwrites readers' real-life stories of hope, comfort, and inspiration.

Twitter: @TanyaBlessings

facebook.com/TanyaRichardsonBlessings